I0816667

THE NEGRONI

CAMPARI
Bitter
Bitter
CAMPARI
DOPO LA TERRA.....GLI ASTRI

THE NEGRONI

A LOVE AFFAIR WITH A CLASSIC COCKTAIL

MATT HRANEK

ARTISAN | NEW YORK

Library of Congress Cataloging-in-Publication Data.

Names: Hranek, Matt, author.
Title: The Negroni / Matt Hranek.
Description: New York : Artisan, a division of Workman Publishing Co., Inc. [2021] | Includes bibliographical references and index.
Identifiers: LCCN 2020042987 | ISBN 9781579659646
Subjects: LCSH: Cocktails. | LCGFT: Cookbooks.
Classification: LCC TX951 .H73 2021 | DDC 641.87/4—dc23
LC record available at https://lccn.loc.gov/2020042987

Design by Headcase Design
Photographs by Matt Hranek, except as noted below:
Page 23: Archivio Cameraphoto/Sonic Editions; page 25: Robertstock; pages 40–41, 49, 52–53, 56, 64–65, 72–73, 77, 81, 96–97, 134–35: Stephen Ringer; pages 60–61, 110-11: Todd Ritondaro; page 91: Gary Harrison; page 118: Steve Freihon; page 152: Yolanda Edwards; page 160: Clara Hranek

Published by Artisan
A division of Workman Publishing Co., Inc.
225 Varick Street
New York, NY 10014-4381
artisanbooks.com

Printed in China on responsibly sourced paper

10 9 8 7 6

To all the barkeepers around the globe
who have taught me, served me,
and guided me on the journey
with this fantastic drink

CONTENTS

BAR
SERVIZIO

PREFACE

A guy walks into a bar. A Florentine bar, actually. He takes a seat and orders an Americano, a straightforward drink with a nice balance of bitter (Campari) and sweet (red vermouth), served over ice. But this isn't just any guy. He happens to be a well-traveled Italian count who, after spending some time in Holland as well as in England, has developed a taste for gin. So, as the barman makes his drink, he tells him to lose the splash of soda (the usual topper of the Americano) and replace it with gin. The barman obliges, and in a final flourish, replaces the lemon garnish with a slice of orange. That is the basic story of the birth of the Negroni, named for the count himself.

That's not the only story, however, as these things go. There are at least a couple of other origin theories for the Negroni that dispute it. But the story that most Negroni scholars agree on is the one above, tracing the drink back to 1919 Florence and the Caffè Casoni, where it was named for its creator (or biggest fan), Count Camillo Negroni. Let's leave it at that. This book is less a historical treatise than a celebration of the drink itself, and of my enthusiasm for it.

My love for the Negroni goes deep. I fell hard for the first one I tried, decades ago, in an Italian hotel whose name didn't stick with me the way the memory of the drink did. It was served to me as part of the hotel's *aperitivo* (the Italian tradition of a drink and light snack that serves as a precursor to dinner—think happy hour). The Negroni spoke to me. I was attracted to its color, its flavor, and, most of all, its perfect balance: equal parts gin (dry, with a hint of botanicals and juniper), vermouth (a spicy touch of sweetness), and Campari (the delightfully bitter finish), as well as the citrusy notes from the orange garnish.

When I was growing up, my family drank wine with meals, to be social and celebratory, not to get drunk. My mother's parents emigrated from the south of Italy as teens, and my grandfather made his own wine. He served it to everyone, including us kids. He'd drop a thimbleful into our water, which turned it slightly purple. Those first drinking experiences shaped my habits as an adult. Sure, I have had a drink catch up with me, and have even drowned a few sorrows in one (or several), but drinking will always be a positive, joyous act for me.

I've come a long way from my grandfather's watered-down wine, and the Negroni is now one of my two drinks of choice when I travel, and when I'm at home, too. (The other, depending on the location and the circumstance, is the martini.) I have mixed Negronis at home and at friends' houses, in cities and out in the middle of the countryside. I've consumed them in countless bars, restaurants, and airport lounges. I have had spectacular ones (this typically has to do with the location, and, as with many of my other pursuits, the Italians simply do it better). I've tasted some mediocre ones, though even they were good.

There is rarely such a thing as a bad Negroni, which may hold the key to its popularity. The 1:1:1 ratio of ingredients makes it nearly foolproof (and without the soda of the Americano, or any other nonalcoholic mixer, it can feel full-proof). Wherever you find yourself, chances are you can find a bartender who can pour a decent Negroni, even if you have to teach them the ratio. (I've been known to give Negroni-making lessons to flight attendants in the galleys of planes.)

The Negroni is also consumed as a digestif at the end of a meal. A few years ago, I made a short film about Alessandro Palazzi of Dukes Bar in London, a barman legendary for his delicious if somewhat deadly martinis, and his Negronis as well. Over the course of filming, I went over the house limit of two Vesper martinis per customer, and so proceeded to try to crawl

SSPORT
United States
of America
BOARDING PASS

my way home once the shoot wrapped. I ran into friends on the way out the door, however, and they insisted I stick around for one more drink. I ended that evening the way I ordinarily begin so many others, with a Negroni, but this time for its digestive assistance as much as its taste.

I now have more photos of Negronis I've enjoyed around the world than of my family (I am not so proud of that fact). Most of them have populated my social media feed. The Negroni is a big part of my photo sharing, and as a result, people from all over tag me in photos of their own Negronis.

It's fair to say that I have strong opinions about the Negroni. Generally, I do not deviate from ordering the standard recipe of one part bitter Campari, one part sweet vermouth, one part gin (for me, that's always London dry). That being said, I do approve of some riffs and modifications—within moderation, of course. I've been introduced to some fantastic versions by friends and fellow travelers, and I've even (though rarely) been convinced to give a bartender creative license. Often the drinks that I've been most dubious about have won me over. All of those variations—the slight deviations and a few outright reinterpretations—are included in this book. All come from some of my favorite places and people around the world. And yes, all have been field-tested by me.

If you've never tried a Negroni, I hope you will fall in love with this remarkable drink the way I did decades ago in that Italian hotel. If you are already a fellow aficionado, as I suspect you may be since you are holding this book in your hands, I hope it inspires you to try a new twist, seek out a few of my favorite bars and bartenders, and continue to celebrate the beautiful balance of this drink. Although you really can't improve much on the original that Count Negroni invented that day in Florence, that doesn't mean you can't enjoy the pursuit. *Salute!*

"CAMPARI,"
l'aperitivo

The ESSENTIAL COMPONENTS

The Negroni is famously democratic in its makeup, with each of its three essential components traditionally represented in equal measure. With few exceptions, a garnish and some ice fill out the glass. Here are a few considerations for each.

"The bitters are excellent for your liver, the gin is bad for you. They balance each other."

—ORSON WELLES

THE BITTER

Aperitif bitters should not be confused with the bitters sold in small bottles, the ones that are dashed into some of our other favorite cocktails. These Italian bitters have been produced regionally throughout the country for more than a century. They begin as wine or a neutral spirit, which is first infused with various botanicals—including herbs, spices, and fruit—and then dyed red. (Originally the crushed shells of the cochineal beetle were used to achieve the red color; now other natural and artificial colorings are used.) A cocktail featuring one of these bitters is the drink of choice before dinner, along with a bite to eat to stimulate the appetite. (I usually have no problem stimulating my appetite while in Italy, by the way.) Because the alcohol content of most bitters varies from 20 to 28.5%, they also pack a bit of a punch, so pairing a bitters-based cocktail with food is always a good idea for pacing purposes.

Italian bitters are not one-note. Their flavor is best described as bitter and sweet at once. The botanical infusions give each blend (and brand) a distinctive taste, which can include hints of orange, rhubarb, clove, vanilla, and anise (licorice), to name just a few familiar flavor notes. Exact ingredients and formulas are closely guarded secrets. The most well-known aperitif bitter is Campari, created by Gaspare Campari in Novara, a town in the Piedmont region in 1860. Later, his son Davide was responsible for its worldwide distribution. As Italian bitters have increased in popularity in recent years, more and more small distilleries—even in the United States—are in the business of creating their own variations.

The following are some of my favorite bitters.

- Bèrto
- Campari
- Contratto Bitter
- Galliano
- Luxardo Bitter
- Martini Riserva
- Meletti 1870
- Peychaud
- Rinomato
- St. Agrestis Inferno Bitter
- Tassoni

THE VERMOUTH

One pivotal factor in determining the proper balance of a Negroni is the choice of vermouth, more so than the gin (for more on gin, see page 22). Its style and producer can completely change the way a Negroni tastes.

Vermouth is not a spirit but a neutral wine fortified with additional alcohol (brandy or eau-de-vie, typically), aromatized with various botanicals, and sweetened with sugar (cane or caramelized). It finds its origins in eighteenth-century Turin, Italy. Botanicals, which were chosen originally for their medicinal properties as well as their flavors, vary by producer. Most blends consist of herbs (marjoram, coriander, and hyssop, among many others), spices (clove, cinnamon, ginger, juniper, and cardamom are just a few), citrus peels, tree bark, and plant roots and shrubs, which give vermouth its name. (The term is a bastardization of the German word *Wermut*, or wormwood, a shrub commonly thought to aid digestion and cure multiple ailments.) As with aperitif bitters, the specific combinations of flavoring agents in vermouth were highly protected among early manufacturers, and remain so today.

Vermouth can be sweet (red) or dry (white). Although there are no hard-and-fast rules about where it can be produced, sweet vermouth is the Italian original, and dry hails from France, where it was introduced by the Noilly family in the early nineteenth century. It was not until the late nineteenth century that vermouth became popular with bartenders as an aperitif and

PUNT E MES

aperitivo Carpano

TESTA

as a key ingredient in classic cocktails like the martini (and the Manhattan).

The Italian red vermouths are used in Negronis. Carpano makes some great ones, like Antica Formula, and my go-to, Punt e Mes ("point and a half" in English), which is rich, spicy, and aromatic with notes of orange pith, mint, and cinnamon. Its name comes from its formula: one point sweetness and a half point bitterness. I like the hints of vanilla in Cinzano and Cocchi. Martini & Rossi, which is widely available, is acceptable in a pinch.

Some of the French vermouths, like Dolin, are nice, but to me, using a French vermouth in a classic Negroni is sacrilege. There are now also some small-batch vermouth producers, including American and Spanish companies, but the choice is a matter of personal taste. Just as you may slightly tweak the proportions of the spirits that make up this fine cocktail, you may also vary the type of vermouth you use. Drink what you like, how you like it.

THE GIN

The gin, of course, is crucial to the character of Negronis past and present. The story of gin starts in the Netherlands, with the spirit genever. (The name comes from the Dutch word for juniper; it's also sometimes known as jenever, Hollands, or Dutch gin.) This crudely distilled spirit begins with malt wine; botanicals and herbs, including a good dose of its namesake juniper, are added to make it more palatable. Genever is sometimes considered a type of gin, or the original gin, but that's not quite accurate.

Early versions of genever were more like whiskey than the gin we know today. Like many liquors, it was used for medicinal purposes (juniper was believed to have healing properties) as far back as the sixteenth century. British soldiers discovered it while fighting various wars in the Netherlands around the same time. After the wars, they brought genever back to England, where it gained popularity over the next hundred years or so. During that time, the British began to distill spirits of their own, including their version of genever, which they shortened to "gin." The result is the clear, juniper-forward, more-neutral grain alcohol known as London dry gin.

As noted earlier, London dry is my gin of choice for a Negroni. I like the sweet pine and soft citrus notes, as well as the complexity of the botanicals and the rooty finish. I would never use a flavored gin, such as one that is lemony or cucumber-forward, in my Negroni, lest I throw off that perfect balance. There is a long list of commercially available London dry gins—now more than ever, in fact, as small distilleries proliferate all over the world.

My go-to gin choices include the following.

- Beefeater
- Berry Bros. & Rudd No. 3
- Bombay
- Botanist
- Monkey 47
- Plymouth
- Sipsmith
- Tanqueray

Ernest Hemingway, behind a bar counter, pouring gin from a bottle of Gordon's, Cortina d'Ampezzo, Italy, 1948

If I'm in Brooklyn, I'll often opt for one of the local favorites, like Dorothy Parker or Brooklyn gin. While in upstate New York, I'll have Prohibition gin.

Finally, although it may go without saying, I'll say it anyway: I would *never* substitute vodka for gin in a Negroni. If there is vodka on hand but no gin, I'll make another drink, and you should, too. God knows there are loads of them to choose from.

THE GARNISH

I garnish my Negronis with a slice or wedge of orange. I am not that particular about the orange, though; it doesn't have to be organic, for example, or imported from Sicily. I have used blood oranges in season and even a lemon on a few desperate occasions when an orange was not at hand. There are recipes in this book whose creators specify orange peel over a slice, or a lemon twist, or even a grapefruit "coin" (which is just a round of peel). When I make any of their versions, I respect their wishes, but for me, the garnish of choice will always be a slice from that old reliable standard, the Florida orange. I prefer the orange slice or wedge because that is how old-school Italian bartenders do it, and how my first Negroni was served to me.

THE ICE

I don't obsess over the ice. Ideally, it's big, clear cubes, but I realize that this is not always a possibility, so I use whatever's on hand. Once when I was making Negronis for friends, I drove all over the rural south of France trying to find ice for sale. (My friends didn't even have ice trays to make their own.) I managed to find a few cubes floating in an ice bucket at a small village bar and bought them. (They are not big on ice in that region of France.) Use what you have.

CINZANO
VERMOUTH TORINO

The EQUIPMENT

The Negroni has a lot to recommend it, not least the lack of equipment necessary to make a great one. Here are the very few items required.

GLASSWARE

Order a Negroni in a bar, and you're most likely to be handed one in an old-fashioned glass. That said, variations abound, and some bartenders take license with the choice of glassware. Again, the beauty of this cocktail is in its utter simplicity. Use whatever you have at home, as long as it can hold the ice and the rest of the ingredients. If a recipe calls for a chilled glass, place it in the freezer for 10 minutes or so, or fill it with ice and water and toss that out just before you mix your drink.

OLD-FASHIONED GLASS

This is the most commonly used vessel for Negronis. I have many dedicated Negroni glasses that I have collected over the years, some of which I've picked up in flea markets, along with a few from Baccarat. I love the density and weight of crystal glasses, which make the drink feel more important and special. That doesn't mean I am going to let a plain old-fashioned glass—or a paper coffee cup, for that matter—get in the way of my enjoying a Negroni.

COUPE

I love discovering coupes out in the wild, at flea markets, and in antique shops. The vintage ones are, in my opinion, often the best, and you can usually find them cheap.

HIGHBALL GLASS

This is a taller, narrower version of the old-fashioned glass.

NICK & NORA GLASS

This stemmed, bell-shaped glass is wider than a wineglass but not quite as wide as a martini glass or coupe. It's named for Nick and Nora Charles, the characters in Dashiell Hammett's novel *The Thin Man* (and the film series that followed).

BARWARE

Beyond the mix of spirits and the garnish, you can make a decent Negroni with little more than a glass and some ice. That said, some of the variations in this book require a tool or two from the bartender's standard arsenal.

JIGGER

A jigger is pretty much anything you can use to measure the proportions of your Negroni. Since making a proper one is all about balance, just be sure to keep it 1:1:1 (unless otherwise specified in the recipe). Jiggers can be decorative and elegant, or simple and utilitarian. To be honest, I rarely use a jigger myself, preferring instead to eyeball amounts.

BAR SPOON

There are "pro" versions with long, spiraled handles, as well as copper and silver bar spoons. But I often just use the knife that I cut the orange slice with, or even the slice itself, to swirl the ingredients around in my drink. Or you might take a cue from the late legendary bartender and cocktail authority Gary Regan and use your index finger.

MIXING GLASS OR SHAKER

There are lots of options here, from the finest Baccarat crystal to a professional stainless steel model to a Mason jar in a pinch. All of them will work.

STRAINER

Pick up a short-handled bar strainer if you don't already have one; they're more presentable and easier to use than a standard kitchen strainer.

PEELER

To remove a strip of citrus peel, use a standard vegetable peeler. Work the peeler around the fruit, following the curve and using a light hand to avoid picking up any of the bitter white pith. If you don't have a peeler, a sharp knife will do. Keep the pressure even so that the strip is uniformly thick, and scrape off any of the pith that clings to the peel.

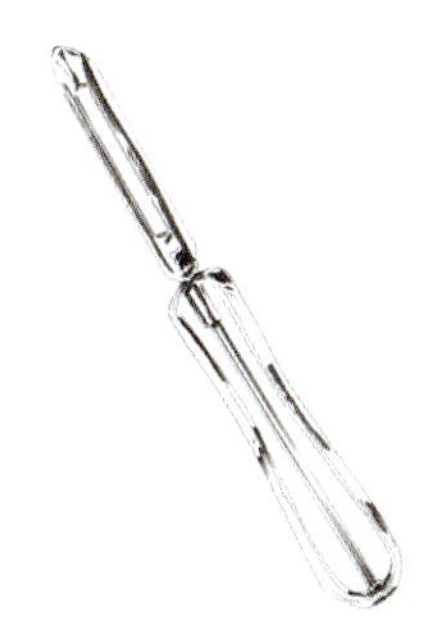

FISA 57
Bitter
CAMPARI
CAMPARI
apéritif

The RECIPES

"[The Negroni] has the power, rare with drinks and indeed with anything else, of cheering you up."

—KINGSLEY AMIS,
Everyday Drinking

CAMPARI
Bitter
MPARI
ordial
CAMPARI
Bitter
Cordial
un vero liquor
con una sfum
CAMPARI
Soda
CAMPA

With two exceptions, the recipes that follow are designed to make one Negroni. All can be doubled or otherwise scaled up to serve more than one. Generally, you can mix the ingredients up to several hours ahead and store them in the refrigerator for later. Wait until just before serving to add ice and garnishes.

The first recipe represents my preferences for ingredients and their proportions. From there, the recipes are arranged by country and region. Most of the components are easy to find, but if you need to substitute one type of sweet vermouth, say, for another, by all means do so. Likewise, if you don't have the exact glass or perfect ice, please improvise. The point is to inspire you to pour yourself a drink and enjoy it.

THE AUTHOR'S NEGRONI

Wm Brown Farm, New York

My house cocktail deviates slightly from the 1:1:1 formula, leaning heavier on the Campari and gin and lighter on the vermouth than the classic version. Good ice is not as important to me as a good glass, and the choice is always crystal, preferably something from my Baccarat collection.

- **1¼ ounces (40 ml) Campari**
- **1¼ ounces (40 ml) London dry gin**
- **¾ ounce (20 ml) Punt e Mes vermouth**
- **Slice of orange for garnish**

Combine the Campari, gin, and vermouth in an old-fashioned glass filled with ice. Stir and garnish with the orange slice.

THE AMERICANO

Camparino in Galleria, Milan

The story of the Negroni begins with this precursor, traced back to 1860 and Gaspare Campari's bar in Milan. The Americano was originally known as the Milano-Torino (Milano is the birthplace of Campari, and Torino that of vermouth). Some say its name change was sparked by its popularity with American expats in Italy; others claim that it was named in honor of Primo Carnera, an Italian boxer who was nicknamed "the Americano" after winning a world championship at Madison Square Garden in 1933.

- **1 ounce (30 ml) Campari**
- **1 ounce (30 ml) sweet vermouth**
- **Soda water**
- **Strip of lemon peel for garnish**

Combine the Campari and vermouth in an old-fashioned glass filled with ice. Top off with a splash of soda water, stir, and garnish with the lemon peel.

"A Negroni—easy to make, delicious to taste, potent in effect: one of life's most agreeable pleasures this side of the law."

—ALEXANDER KRAFT,

entrepreneur

Hotel Il Pellicano, Porto Ercole

THE NEGRONI SBAGLIATO

Bar Basso, Milan

Milan is the birthplace of the Sbagliato ("mistaken") Negroni, with the gin replaced by sparkling wine. The story goes that a bartender at the city's famed Bar Basso accidentally grabbed a bottle of Prosecco instead of gin when making a Negroni for a customer. Before he could retrieve the drink and correct the mistake, the patron stopped him with a "Wait, let's give it a try!" And just like that, the Sbagliato was born.

- **1 ounce (30 ml) sweet vermouth**
- **1 ounce (30 ml) Campari**
- **1 ounce (30 ml) Prosecco or other Italian sparkling white wine**
- **Slice of orange for garnish**

Pour the vermouth, Campari, and Prosecco into a stemmed glass, or other glass of your choice, filled with ice. Stir and garnish with the orange slice.

IL COCKTAIL
MODERNO
Bar Basso
TEL. 29400580

Basso
GNE
ANT

"It's the bitter aspect of the Negroni that always makes me come back for more. I don't love overly sweet cocktails, and this classic Italian flirts nicely with that idea."

—BRAD LEONE,

video personality

THE WILLIAM BROWN NEGRONI

Hotel Il Pellicano, Porto Ercole, Italy

As with real estate, sometimes the most important factor in determining the enjoyment of a Negroni comes down to one word: location. For me, nowhere is that more evident than at the bar of the Hotel Il Pellicano in Porto Ercole, on the Tuscan coast. There is something about the caught-in-time elegance, the view of the sea from the cliff top, and the expertise and charm of the head barman, Federico Morosi, that makes it a singular experience. Federico considers the Negroni a symbol of Italy, especially of Florence—like a bespoke suit in its *eleganza* and singular character. He enjoys the drink just as much with a square of dark chocolate and a superb Tuscan cigar after dinner as with salty snacks during the *aperitivo* hour. In this house specialty, which Federico graciously named in honor of my Wm Brown brand, an intensely flavored, golden-colored aperitif known as Biancosarti stands in for the sweet vermouth. The result is a bright, blond variation on the original.

- **1 ounce (30 ml) Campari**
- **1 ounce (30 ml) Tuscan gin**
- **1 ounce (30 ml) Biancosarti**
- **Strip of lemon peel for garnish**
- **Strip of orange peel for garnish**

Combine the Campari, gin, and Biancosarti in an old-fashioned glass filled with ice. Stir and garnish with the citrus peels.

"A Negroni, like many wonderful creations, is deceptively simple. When it's done absolutely right—when you have that huge ice cube, the fresh orange peel, and that delicate balance of flavors of the right components in a sturdy glass—it's a drink that's not only delicious but seems made to carry you through great conversations and memories."

—AZIZ ANSARI,

writer/director/actor/comedian/Negroni fan

RISTORANTE

THE TELLER

Hotel Il Pellicano, Porto Ercole, Italy

Another of Il Pellicano's house cocktails (see page 50), this variation is named for Juergen Teller, the German fine-art and fashion photographer who has spent his fair share of time at the hotel bar. His namesake Negroni is finished with a splash of Chinotto soda, Italy's herbaceous, sweet-bitter counterpart to American Coca-Cola.

- 1 ounce (30 ml) Carpano Antica Formula vermouth
- 1 ounce (30 ml) Campari
- 1 ounce (30 ml) Plymouth gin
- Splash of Chinotto
- Slice of orange for garnish

Combine the vermouth, Campari, and gin in an old-fashioned glass filled with ice. Top off with the Chinotto, stir, and garnish with the orange slice.

IL PROFESSORE

Grand Hotel Vesuvio, Naples

I love the lobby of the Grand Hotel Vesuvio, with its wonderful three-seat bar (pictured on page 146), which looks more like an Italian living room than a reception area. Antonio the barman is a slow reveal—reserved and serious when you make his acquaintance, then eventually becoming the most vivacious, loquacious version of himself once you get him going on the subject of Negronis. He adds a touch of coffee liqueur (and a few coffee beans) to this variation, which caught me by surprise in its deliciousness.

- 1 ounce (30 ml) gin
- 1 ounce (30 ml) Campari
- 1 ounce (30 ml) sweet vermouth
- ⅓ ounce (10 ml) coffee liqueur (preferably a small-batch Italian version; otherwise, Kahlúa is fine)
- Slice of orange for garnish
- Coffee beans for garnish (optional)

Combine the gin, Campari, vermouth, and coffee liqueur in an old-fashioned glass filled with ice. Stir and garnish with the orange slice and coffee beans, if using.

Piazza Navona in Rome

IL CHIERICHETTO

Belmond Grand Hotel Timeo, Sicily

I have Alfio Liotta, the former bar manager of Belmond Grand Hotel Timeo in Taormina, to thank for this variation. To Alfio, preparing a Negroni in just the right way is almost a religious act, which inspired him to create his own signature cocktail, Il Chierichetto, Italian for "the altar boy." The bitter artichoke flavor of the Cynar works beautifully with the rich, deeply flavorful Cocchi vermouth and the super-citrusy O de V Chinotto.

- **1 ounce (30 ml) O de V Chinotto**
- **1 ounce (30 ml) Cynar**
- **1 ounce (30 ml) Cocchi Storico Vermouth di Torino**
- **Strip of orange peel for garnish**
- **Strip of lemon peel for garnish**

Combine the Chinotto, Cynar, and vermouth in an old-fashioned glass filled with ice. Stir and garnish with the citrus peels.

"I remember being so young, and working at my father's friend's bar during the school summer break. When the bartender found me spying on him while he was preparing cocktails, he told me, 'Come here. Take a short tumbler, fill it with ice, and pour in one part Campari, one part Carpano sweet vermouth, and one part Gordon's gin. Begin always with the Campari and finish with the gin. We are making a Negroni!'"

—ALFIO LIOTTA,

bar ambassador at Me Cumpari Turiddu, Catania, Sicily

BARREL-AGED NEGRONIS WITH DRIED FIGS

Thalami, Patmos, Greece

My wife loves Greece, so I am in tow to the islands every summer. After many liters of Greek beer and wine, though, I start to go through Negroni withdrawal. Thankfully, my friend Gregoris introduced me to Thalami, an oasis of a bar on the island of Patmos. The owner-bartender, George, is a master craftsman, and he puts a very Greek spin on his barrel-aged Negronis by steeping the spirits with dried figs. Follow the basic template below to make as many Negronis as you wish.

- **1 part Campari**
- **1 part gin**
- **1 part vermouth**
- **A handful of dried figs**
- **Orange slices for garnish**

Pour the spirits into a bottle (or barrel) and stir in the dried figs. Seal the vessel and let the mixture steep for at least a few days. Serve the Negronis over ice, garnished with orange slices.

The Castel dell'Ovo on the Gulf of Naples

IL NEGRONI VECCHIO

I have been collecting vintage bottles of Campari and other bitters, vermouth, and gin for years. I look for them at old-school Italian bars and at shops when I travel around Europe, hoping to unearth a bottle from the 1950s, '60s, or '70s. Admittedly, these are hard to find, but well worth it if you can get your hands on one of them. The original Campari recipe was more bitter, less sweet. When I combine these old spirits in the Negroni Vecchio (the "old Negroni"), it's like taking a sip back in time.

- **1 ounce (30 ml) vintage Campari**
- **1 ounce (30 ml) vintage sweet vermouth**
- **1 ounce (30 ml) gin, preferably vintage**
- **Slice of orange for garnish**

Combine the Campari, vermouth, and gin in an old-fashioned glass filled with ice. Stir and garnish with the orange slice.

PUNT E MES
CARPANO
PUNT E MES
VERMOUTH AMARO
DELL'ANTICA FABBRICA
G. B. CARPANO
TORINO
PALAZZO CARPANO
SI BEVE FREDDO
MILANO
CAMPARI
CAMPARI
Cont. 1 litro
Bitter
G. Campari
FRATELLI CAMPARI

Ristorante

PIAZZA DEL POPOLO
ATI
Caffetteria

EL NEGRONI DE JUÁREZ

Hotel Vilòn, Rome

It's not often that you run into a female bartender in Italy, so I was surprised to see Magdalena Rodriguez, a native of Costa Rica, behind the bar at the Hotel Vilòn in Rome. The hotel is down a small street in the center of the city, steps from the Trevi Fountain and overlooking the gardens of the Palazzo Borghese. Magdalena convinced me to try this creative take on the Negroni, including smoky mezcal; Rinomato, a lesser-known Italian red bitter; and Fernet-Branca, the well-known and well-loved amaro.

- **1 ounce (30 ml) mezcal**
- **1 ounce (30 ml) Rinomato bitter**
- **1 ounce (30 ml) Cocchi Storico Vermouth di Torino**
- **2 drops Fernet-Branca**
- **Slices of orange for garnish**

Combine the mezcal, bitter, vermouth, and Fernet-Branca in an old-fashioned glass filled with ice. Stir and garnish with the orange slices.

"What is so damn good about a Negroni is what I would call its simple complexity. It is a very easy to make drink consisting of three ingredients in equal amounts poured directly into a glass, then stirred and topped with an orange twist. But it is the complexity of the way these three ingredients interact with and affect one another that makes a Negroni one of the kings of the mixed drinks."

—PAUL FEIG,

Hollywood director, writer, and producer and creator of Artingstall's Brilliant London Dry Gin

MARTINI
Caffè
Torino
Ristorante
LAUDER

Sant Eustachio
il caffè

LA REINA DE ROCA

Hotel Vilòn, Rome

I told Magdalena Rodriguez (see page 74) outright that I was *very* skeptical about this drink when she suggested it (chocolate bitters?), but as proof that I am not completely made of stone, I trusted her and agreed to try it. I was impressed by its perfect balance of flavors. It's not something I would order as an aperitif, but it's certainly a good way to end an evening. Magdalena uses lemon gin, which she creates herself by steeping lemon peels in gin for up to two days (no longer).

- **1 ounce (30 ml) lemon gin, store-bought or homemade (see above)**
- **1 ounce (30 ml) Riserva Carlo Alberto Bitter Rouge**
- **2 dashes Fee Brothers Aztec chocolate bitters**
- **2 to 3 dashes fresh lemon juice**
- **Strip of lemon peel for garnish**
- **Dehydrated orange wheel for garnish**

Combine the gin, both bitters, and lemon juice in an old-fashioned glass filled with ice. Stir and garnish with the lemon peel and dehydrated orange wheel.

THE BUÑUELONI

This variation on the classic Negroni comes from the late avant-garde surrealist Spanish filmmaker Luis Buñuel. He cited his preference for this gin-forward, double-vermouth predinner cocktail in his 1982 memoir, *My Last Sigh*.

- **3 ounces (90 ml) gin**
- **1 ounce (30 ml) Cinzano or Martini & Rossi Rosso**
- **1 ounce (30 ml) Punt e Mes or Carpano Classico vermouth**
- **Slice of orange for garnish**

Combine the gin, Cinzano, and vermouth in a highball glass filled with ice. Stir and garnish with the orange slice.

THE RUM NEGRONI

I'm generally a location rum drinker: I'll drink it in the Caribbean, but if I'm anywhere else in the world, chances are I won't reach for a bottle. Certainly not when I'm in Italy. Yet in this drink, the rum is a delightful surprise. Since it doesn't pack quite the punch of the classic (rum is more gentle than gin), this might be a good gateway for the ordinarily Negroni-averse. Make sure to choose a good dark rum, rather than light rum, for the most complex flavor. I'm especially fond of the rums from Mount Gay, the world's oldest rum distillery, in operation on the island of Barbados since 1703.

- **1 ounce (30 ml) Mount Gay rum**
- **1 ounce (30 ml) Campari**
- **1 ounce (30 ml) sweet vermouth**
- **Slice of orange for garnish**

Combine the rum, Campari, and vermouth in an old-fashioned glass filled with ice. Stir and garnish with the orange slice.

MOUNT GAY®
Barbados Rum EST. 1703
XO
TRIPLE CASK BLEND

The Mount Gay distillery in Barbados

THE AMBER NEGRONI

The name for this variation comes from the substitution of caramel-colored amaro for the usual red Campari. I like this drink with Cynar (made from artichokes and other plants), which gives the flavor profile an appealing bitterness. In fact, I like Cynar so much that it's often my drink of choice when I'm almost—but not quite—ready to call it a night. I'll order a Cynar with lemon and soda so I can stay in good form while enjoying the company and conversation of friends as they continue to knock 'em back.

- **1 ounce (30 ml) gin**
- **1 ounce (30 ml) amaro, preferably Cynar**
- **1 ounce (30 ml) sweet vermouth**
- **Slice of orange for garnish**

Combine the gin, amaro, and vermouth in an old-fashioned glass filled with ice. Stir and garnish with the orange slice.

THE LONDINIUM NEGRONI

Dukes Bar, London

Down a nondescript street in Mayfair, you will find London's famed Dukes. Bar manager Alessandro Palazzi, an Italian by birth, is an undisputed master of his craft, known the world over for his signature Vesper martini. It is meticulously composed and famously lethal (there's a strictly enforced two-martini limit). Ask Alessandro to name his drink of choice, however, and he'll admit to a preference for the Negroni. His distinctly English riff, which features the classic 1:1:1 balance, is made with Sacred Spirits, handcrafted in a small-batch distillery in Highgate.

- **1 ounce (30 ml) Sacred Spirits gin**
- **1 ounce (30 ml) Sacred Spirits rosehip cup liqueur**
- **1 ounce (30 ml) Sacred Spirits spiced vermouth**
- **Slice of orange for garnish**

Combine the gin, liqueur, and vermouth in an old-fashioned glass filled with ice. Stir and garnish with the orange slice.

S

HARRY'S BAR
FIRENZE
HARRY'S BAR
FIRENZE

STVDJ DI PITTVRA
E DI

THE ORIGINAL
GORDON'S
LONDON DRY GIN
IAN FLEMING
FOR YOUR EYES ONLY
A SIGNET BOOK COMPLETE AND UNABRIDGED
5 JAMES BOND THRILLERS

THE SPECIAL AGENT NEGRONI

While the martini is James Bond's drink of choice, he orders a Negroni in "Risico," one of the short stories in Ian Fleming's book *For Your Eyes Only*. This recipe is inspired by that drink. Bond always specified Gordon's gin for his order.

- **1 ounce (30 ml) Gordon's gin**
- **1 ounce (30 ml) Campari**
- **1 ounce (30 ml) sweet vermouth**
- **Slice of orange for garnish**

Combine the gin, Campari, and vermouth in an old-fashioned glass filled with ice. Stir and garnish with the orange slice.

THE FERGRONI

St. John Bread and Wine, London

There are not many bottled Negroni mixes I can recommend other than that from one of my favorite British chefs, Fergus Henderson. At his restaurant St. John Bread and Wine, you can order two types of Negroni, the classic version and another that isn't actually listed on the menu, made the way Fergus himself drinks it. It's called the Fergroni (aka "the Negroni as it should be") and was originally ordered only by those in the know. Now the Fergroni is accessible to all in a commercially bottled blend, but it's easy to replicate at home.

- **1½ ounces (45 ml) Tanqueray gin**
- **1 ounce (30 ml) Punt e Mes vermouth**
- **½ ounce (15 ml) Campari**
- **Strip of lemon peel (strictly no orange) for garnish**

Combine the gin, vermouth, and Campari in an old-fashioned glass filled with ice. Stir and garnish with the lemon peel.

FERGUS

"The Negroni has been a long-standing cocktail companion of mine. The hour of the aperitif is not complete without one! It is a drink with rigor—to be consumed with responsibility. Serve always with a strip of lemon zest (never orange)."

—FERGUS HENDERSON,

chef and cofounder, St. John Restaurant

"As a teenager, I was a huge fan of Marguerite Duras's novel Les petits chevaux de Tarquinia. *Her characters, on vacation in a small Italian village, spend their time drinking bitter Campari. Campari truly becomes a recurring character in the novel. After reading the book, I too started to enjoy Campari. From there, the Negroni became my favorite cocktail. If I don't remember where I drank a Negroni for the first time, I do know that it is the cocktail I order first in every bar I walk into."*

—FRANCK AUDOUX,

owner, Cravan

LE BRISTOL
PARIS

THE LE BRISTOL PARIS NEGRONI

Paris

Le Bristol is certainly one of the most elegant hotels in Paris—old-school but not old-fashioned. On a recent trip, I enjoyed their pre-bottled Negroni from room service, and, lucky for me, was privy to the testing with barman Thierry Hernandez. Each arrives chilled in a glass flask, with a glass, some ice, and a slice of orange. The balance and temperature are perfection.

- **1¼ ounces (40 ml) Tanqueray 10 gin**
- **1¼ ounces (40 ml) Martini & Rossi Vermouth Riserva Speciale Rubino**
- **1¼ ounces (40 ml) Campari**
- **Slice of orange for garnish**

Combine the gin, bitters, and Campari in a mixing glass or cocktail shaker. If you want to re-create Le Bristol's method, funnel the mixture into a flask and store in the fridge for later use. To serve, pour the mixture over ice in the glass of your choice and garnish with the orange slice.

THE TUNNEL

Cravan, Paris

Cravan is a magical little bijoux bar in the 16th Arrondissement, named for Arthur Cravan, the Swiss-born Dadaist artist, poet, and boxer. Shortly after I discovered the bar on a trip to Paris, owner Franck Audoux led me down the path of his excellent Negroni interpretations, including this one, featuring French dry vermouth and a drop of Italian sweet vermouth. "Our variation at Cravan," he says, "has the advantage of making the classic Negroni drier (it is often served too sweet for my taste)." Franck is the author of *French Moderne: Cocktails from the Twenties and Thirties.* To make the "coin" garnish, slice a round of peel off one side of the grapefruit, without cutting into the pith or the fruit.

- **1 ounce (30 ml) gin**
- **1 ounce (30 ml) Noilly Prat dry vermouth**
- **⅔ ounce (20 ml) Campari**
- **⅓ ounce (10 ml) Punt e Mes vermouth**
- **Grapefruit "coin" for garnish (see above)**

Combine the gin, Noilly Prat, Campari, and Punt e Mes in a mixing glass filled with ice. Stir, then strain into a Nick & Nora glass or other glass of your choice. Stir and garnish with the grapefruit coin.

Harry's
Paris
www.harrys-bar.fr

THE BOULEVARDIER

Harry's New York Bar, Paris

Consider this the Negroni for bourbon lovers. The Boulevardier was invented in Paris in the 1920s by the eponymous bar owner Harry MacElhone (the first recipe appears in his book *Barflies and Cocktails*, published in 1927). The cocktail was named in honor of the monthly magazine known as *Boulevardier* (whose publisher, Erskine Gwynne, was a regular drinker of Harry's creation). Honestly, I have a Boulevardier only on the rarest of occasions, as I prefer to drink bourbon straight or in a Manhattan. But I know that people love this cocktail, so I would be remiss not to include it.

- **1 ounce (30 ml) bourbon**
- **1 ounce (30 ml) sweet vermouth**
- **1 ounce (30 ml) Campari**
- **Slice of orange for garnish**

Combine the bourbon, vermouth, and Campari in a cocktail shaker filled with ice. Strain into a chilled coupe and garnish with the orange slice. Alternatively, stir the cocktail in an old-fashioned glass filled with ice and garnish with the orange slice.

THE BOULEVARDIER 29

Cravan, Paris

Owner Franck Audoux's riff on the Boulevardier (page 107) features Cognac in place of the usual bourbon. "I must confess that I am very 'old-school' regarding the Negroni," he says. "I like variation only if it plays on the flavor but keeps the classic structure and ingredients and, of course, if it is perfectly balanced. What seems simple is always extremely difficult to achieve."

- **1 ounce (30 ml) Cognac**
- **1 ounce (30 ml) Dubonnet**
- **2 ounces (60 ml) Dolin Bitter or Campari**
- **Strip of orange peel for garnish**

Combine the Cognac, Dubonnet, and bitter in a mixing glass filled with ice. Stir and strain into an old-fashioned glass. Garnish with the strip of orange peel.

A view of Florence

DAMON BOELTE'S NEGRONI

Grand Army, Brooklyn, New York

My old friend Damon Boelte was quite possibly the first bartender to influence my cocktail choices, back when he was the bar manager at Prime Meats, once a favorite (and now sadly defunct) haunt in Carroll Gardens, Brooklyn. Damon is now the proprietor of Grand Army, an excellent spot with a top-notch raw bar in a nearby neighborhood, serving inspired cocktails. And he's a fellow Negroni devotee. "The thing about the Negroni that I adore is its equality," he says. "I'm an identical twin, and a Gemini, so I've always been a fan of equal parts. The fact that you can swap out each ingredient categorically has made it one of the most historically riffed-on cocktails. Following the formula makes for a wide array of fuckaroundability."

- **1½ ounces (45 ml) gin**
- **½ ounce (15 ml) Dolin Rouge vermouth**
- **½ ounce (15 ml) Carpano Antica Formula vermouth**
- **1 ounce (30 ml) Campari**
- **Slice of orange for garnish**

Combine the gin, both vermouths, and Campari in an old-fashioned glass filled with ice. Stir and garnish with the orange slice.

THE NEGRONI FRAPPÉ

Dante, New York City

Without a doubt, Dante, a venerable Italian outpost operating in the heart of Greenwich Village, has influenced the Negroni game like no other bar. Their pioneering Negroni on tap is inspirational; they also often have a Negroni fountain at events, and so I thank the owner, Linden Pride, for speeding up the process of pairing me with my drink. Dante offers some excellent riffs on the traditional Negroni (recipes for three more follow this one).

- **¾ ounce (20 ml) Beefeater gin**
- **¾ ounce (20 ml) Meletti 1870 Bitter Aperitivo**
- **¾ ounce (20 ml) Carpano Antica Formula vermouth**
- **¾ ounce (20 ml) fresh orange juice**
- **3 dashes orange bitters**
- **Finely grated orange zest for garnish**

Combine the gin, Meletti, vermouth, orange juice, and orange bitters in a cocktail shaker and pour over crushed ice in a footed highball glass. Stir, then cap off with more crushed iced. Garnish with orange zest and serve with a straw.

THE OLD PAL

Dante, New York City

This simple alternative to a traditional Negroni—and the more well-known Boulevardier (page 107)—would not be my first drink of the night, but it might very well be the second, when I'm ready for something new. It's noticeably less sweet than the classic, with Noilly Prat dry vermouth standing in for the Italian sweet (I'll make an exception for the French variety in this case), and rye for the more floral-forward gin.

- **1 ounce (30 ml) Wild Turkey 81 rye**
- **¾ ounce (20 ml) Campari**
- **¾ ounce (20 ml) Noilly Prat dry vermouth**
- **Dehydrated lemon wheel or slice of fresh lemon for garnish**

Combine the rye, Campari, and vermouth in a mixing glass filled with ice; stir and strain over ice in an old-fashioned glass. Garnish with the lemon wheel.

CAFFE'
DANTE

"The Negroni is such a simple cocktail—equal parts gin, vermouth, and bitter. And in this sense, it's almost impossible to make a bad one. The bitter component of the cocktail is usually what pulls you in—especially as this is a taste that is generally acquired, over time, as our palate matures. Once you're hooked on that bitter profile, though, the real fun begins. I've always felt that the true wonder of the Negroni is that sense of discovery you embark upon once you start to unpeel the layers. Swap out the base spirits with mezcal, bourbon, or variants of gin, or exchange sweet or dry vermouth with an ever-increasing variety of Italian bitters; the complexity and variations on the drink are seemingly endless."

—LINDEN PRIDE,

owner, Dante

THE CARDINALE

Dante, New York City

Paler in color and significantly less sweet, the Cardinale is a subtle take on the standard Negroni. I like the combination of the rich, fruity Contratto, a lively mix of twenty-four botanicals; an especially spirited New York gin named for celebrated writer (and legendary drinker) Dorothy Parker; and Lo-Fi, a slightly spicy white vermouth from California.

- **Twist of lemon**
- **1 ounce (30 ml) Dorothy Parker gin**
- **¾ ounce (20 ml) Contratto Bitter**
- **¾ ounce (20 ml) Lo-Fi dry vermouth**
- **Dehydrated lemon wheel or slice of fresh lemon for garnish**

Rub the rim of an old-fashioned glass with the lemon twist: discard it. Combine the gin, bitter, and vermouth in a mixing glass filled with ice; stir and strain over ice in the glass. Garnish with the lemon wheel.

Cardinale
Dante NYC

THE NEGRONI BIANCO

Dante, New York City

Dante's version is one of the only acceptable exceptions to my "no Negroni Bianco" rule. It keeps the standard level of bitterness but has an intriguing herbaceousness that I haven't found elsewhere. Alessio Bianco is a clear Italian sweet vermouth (not to be confused with dry white French vermouths), and Carpano Dry is a spicy, herby, relatively new vermouth with noticeable hints of wormwood. The combination of the two is so interesting that I don't miss the red vermouth here at all, or even the Campari. Other notable ingredients include Brooklyn gin, a hometown spirit flavored with fresh citrus peels and hand-cracked juniper, and quinquina, a bright, slightly bitter French aperitif named for cinchona, the bark originally used in quinine. The optional baby's breath garnish is admittedly unusual, but Dante includes it for the floral, grassy notes it delivers to the finish.

- **Twist of lemon**
- **1 ounce (30 ml) Brooklyn gin**
- **½ ounce (15 ml) Alessio Bianco vermouth**
- **½ ounce (15 ml) Carpano Dry vermouth**
- **1 ounce (30 ml) quinquina aperitif**
- **2 dashes lemon bitters**
- **Dash of verjus**
- **Sprig of baby's breath (optional)**

Rub the rim of a Nick & Nora glass with the lemon twist; discard it. Combine the gin, both vermouths, quinquina, bitters, and verjus in a mixing glass filled with ice. Stir and strain into the glass. Garnish with the baby's breath, if you like.

CAMPAR

"I think the Negroni is the perfect cocktail because it is three liquors that I don't particularly like. I don't like Campari, and I don't like sweet vermouth and I don't particularly love gin. But you put them together with that little bit of orange rind in a perfect setting . . . It's just: It sets you up for dinner, in a way it makes you hungry, sands the edges off the afternoon. In an after dinner, it's settling. It is both aperitif and digestive. It's a rare drink that can do that."

—ANTHONY BOURDAIN,

thirstymag.com

FISTFUL OF DOLLARS

Eight Row Flint, Houston, Texas

If there is one man I would trust with a broad reinterpretation of the Negroni, it is Morgan Weber. As the owner of some of the best restaurants and bars in Houston, he enjoys his fair share of agave-based spirits. He uses some very cool ingredients in this riff, including smoky mezcal in place of the gin, not one but two pomegranate liqueurs (Granada-Vallet bitter, also from Mexico, and Pama), and Tempus Fugit Kina L'Aéro d'Or, an aperitif-style white wine.

- **¾ ounce (20 ml) Espadin mezcal**
- **¾ ounce (20 ml) Granada-Vallet bitter**
- **¾ ounce (20 ml) Pama liqueur**
- **¾ ounce (20 ml) Tempus Fugit Kina L'Aéro d'Or**
- **Strip of grapefruit peel for garnish**

Combine the mezcal, Granada-Vallet, Pama, and wine in an old-fashioned glass filled with ice. Stir and garnish with the grapefruit peel.

BOTANIST
22
CAMPARI
Milano
BITTER

THE TOGRONI

Genius. That was the word that came to mind when I first saw this Negroni application on creator Nicholas O'Connell's Instagram feed. Three mini bottles of spirits (called nips in O'Connell's hometown, Boston) are held together with packing tape to make up the 1:1:1 proportion of the classic Negroni perfectly. (Each mini is roughly one shot, 1⅔ ounces/50 ml.) It's great for on-the-run or on-location Negronis without having to schlep the full bottles around. Like I said, genius.

- **1 mini bottle (50 ml) Campari**
- **1 mini bottle (50 ml) sweet vermouth**
- **1 mini bottle (50 ml) gin**
- **Slice of orange for garnish**

Attach the three bottles together with packing tape. When ready to serve, twist off the caps and pour the Campari, vermouth, and gin into an old-fashioned glass filled with ice. Garnish with the orange slice.

"The Negroni really is perfect. The acid from the wine-y thing balances out the sugar in the Campari, and the spirit gives it enough backbone to get the job done. My favorite Negroni was at the Old Saloon in Emigrant, Montana, closing out a day on the Yellowstone River. There's nothing like pulling out of the water in the middle of summer, having banged up the trout pretty hard, and rolling up to the bar at around Negroni-thirty, with that view of Paradise Valley dancing all gemlike out in front of you. Life is definitely good."

—MORGAN WEBER,

owner/beverage director,
Agricole Hospitality

"I love both the taste of the Negroni and how it unites and galvanizes a community of individuals with a shared taste for style, elegance, and depth. Negroni Time forever!"

—WEI KOH,

founder, *The Rake* and *Revolution* magazines

THE SBAGLIATO ROYALE

I don't know anyone who is as dedicated to the Negroni as I am except for my friend Wei Koh, founder of *The Rake*. We have exchanged dozens of photos of Negronis from the many bars we find ourselves in around the world. He is a key player in the Negroni brotherhood, and I always look forward to enjoying one with him face-to-face. His standard Negroni order is made with Monkey 47 gin or, when available, his friend Paul Feig's Artingstall's gin; here is his version of the Sbagliato (page 42), a variation with Champagne in place of the Prosecco.

- **1 ounce (30 ml) Campari**
- **1 ounce (30 ml) Carpano Antica Formula vermouth**
- **1 ounce (30 ml) Ruinart Blanc de Blancs Champagne**
- **Slice of orange for garnish**

Combine the Campari, vermouth, and Champagne in an old-fashioned glass or a stemmed glass filled with ice. Stir and garnish with the orange slice.

1729
Ruinart®
CHAMPAGNE
BLANC DE BLANCS
BRUT · REIMS · FRANCE
PRODUCED BY CHAMPAGNE RUINART · REIMS · FRANCE · NM-549-003

THE MEZCAL NEGRONI BLANCO

Café Altro Paradiso, New York City

I am very fond of Café Altro Paradiso in Manhattan and the long, welcoming, wood-paneled bar that greets you as you walk in. The menu never disappoints, and it came as no surprise to me that their delicious riff on the Negroni combined the flavors of Latin America and Italy so nicely. Chef Ignacio Mattos was born and raised in Uruguay and trained with Argentine chef Francis Mallmann, another one of my favorites. Ignacio developed his favorite Negroni in collaboration with Yola Mezcal in Los Angeles, and he garnishes it with some Japanese pickled plum and a few drops of oro blanco (a citrus hybrid) oil. Admittedly, those ingredients are hard to come by; feel free to use a strip of grapefruit peel in their place.

- **1½ ounces (45 ml) Yola Mezcal**
- **1 ounce (30 ml) Dolin Blanc vermouth**
- **½ ounce (15 ml) Cocchi Americano aperitif**
- **¼ ounce (7 ml) Salers aperitif**
- **A slice of umeboshi plum and oro blanco oil or a strip of grapefruit peel for garnish**

Combine the mezcal, vermouth, and both aperitifs in a well-chilled coupe or other glass of your choice filled with ice. Stir and garnish as desired.

*"Simple and easy to make,
Negronis are nevertheless
well structured, rounded,
and sophisticated.*

I personally love mezcal, so I developed a version that allows me to have my favorite cocktail and spirit together."

—IGNACIO MATTOS,

chef

PRE-BATCHED NEGRONIS

When I'm packing for a road trip, I usually don't feel like lugging along three separate bottles. To lighten the load, I fill one bottle with pre-batched Negronis. A liter usually suffices, depending on where I'm going and with whom.

- **1 part Campari**
- **1 part London dry gin**
- **1 part sweet vermouth**

Choose a bottle that will last the length of your trip. Using a funnel, fill it with the Campari, gin, and vermouth.

NEGRONI

Vitti

THE SNACKS

When it comes to pairing snacks with Negronis, think all manner of crunchy, salty things. The best Italian bars, like Camparino in Galleria in Milan, have the most amazing variety of such nibbles. Here are some of my favorite options.

- Potato chips (the simpler, the better; Lay's are my favorite)
- Green olives (Cerignola or Castelvetrano)
- Salted nuts (I like Marcona almonds and peanuts)
- Popcorn (I buy an heirloom variety from Wildcraft near my house in upstate New York) with sea salt
- Sliced cucumbers with flaky salt and a squeeze of citrus juice
- Whole radishes with butter and salt
- Firm, salty cheeses like Pecorino
- Panini made with Parma ham
- Pizzette, preferably topped with anchovy or simply a bit of tomato and mozzarella or Pecorino
- Charcuterie: prosciutto, sopressata, mortadella, and/or salami
- Taralli (ring-shaped Italian breadsticks)

The lobby bar at the Grand Hotel Vesuvio

THE BLACK BOOK

Beyond my own home or my friends' homes, my favorite place to have a Negroni is, basically, anywhere in Italy. Generally speaking, I don't recommend places I've never been, bartenders I've never met, or drinks I've never tasted, but I am an enthusiast when it comes to all things Negroni, and open to recommendations of all sorts. If you have a hot tip about a must-try bar or interesting interpretation of this drink, by all means send it my way. Here are a few places that stand out.

France

Cravan
17 Rue Jean de la Fontaine
Paris
+33 1 40 50 14 30
@cravanparis

Hotel Bachaumont
18 Rue Bachaumont
Paris
+33 1 81 66 47 00
hotelbachaumont.com

Harry's New York Bar
5 Rue Daunou
Paris
+33 1 42 61 71 14
facebook.com/
harrysnewyorkbarparis

Le Bar du Bristol
Le Bristol Paris
112 Rue du Faubourg
Saint-Honoré
Paris
+33 1 53 43 43 00
oetkercollection.com/
hotels/le-bristol-paris/
restaurants-bar/#tab-bar

The Shell
Grands Boulevards Hotel
17 Boulevard Poissonnière
Paris
+33 1 85 73 33 32
grandsboulevardshotel.com

Greece

Thalami
Chora 85500
Patmos
+30 698 600 4074
facebook.com/thalami
cocktailbar

Italy

Bar All'Aperto
Hotel Il Pellicano
Località Sbarcatello
Porto Ecole
+39 0564 858111
hotelilpellicano.com/en

Bar Basso
Via Plinio, 39
Milan
+39 02 2940 0580
barbasso.com/en

Belmond Grand Hotel Timeo
Via Teatro Greco, 59
Taormina
+39 0942 627 0200
belmond.com/hotels/europe/italy/taormina/belmond-grand-hotel-timeo

Belmond Hotel Splendido
Salita Baratta, 16
Portofino
+39 0185 2678 01
belmond.com/hotels/europe/italy/portofino/belmond-hotel-splendido

Caffè Gilli
Via Roma, 1r
Florence
+39 055 213896
caffegilli.com

Caffè Torino
Piazza San Carlo, 204
Turin
+39 011 545118
caffetorino-torino.it/bar-e-caffe

Camparino in Galleria
Piazza del Duomo, 21
Milan
+39 02 8646 4435
camparino.com/en

Grand Hotel Tremezzo
Via Regina, 8
Tremezzo
+39 0344 42491
grandhoteltremezzo.com/en/home

Harry's Bar
Lungarno Amerigo Vespucci, 22/R
Florence
+39 055 239 6700
harrysbarfirenze.it/en/harrys

Hotel Vilòn
Via dell'Arancio, 69
Rome
+39 06 87 81 87
hotelvilon.com

La Vesuvietta Bar
Grand Hotel Vesuvio
Via Partenope, 45
Naples
+39 081 764 0044
vesuvio.it/en/bar

Tassoni
Via San Carlo, 28
Salò
cedraltassoni.it/en

Japan

New York Bar
Park Hyatt Tokyo, 52nd Floor
3-7-1-2 Nishi-Shinjuku
Shinjuku-Ku
Tokyo
+81 3 5323 3458
restaurants.tokyo.park.hyatt.co
.jp/en/nyb.html

Switzerland

Grand Hotel Les Trois Rois
Blumenrain 8
Basel
+41 61 260 50 50
lestroisrois.com/en

Kulm Hotel
Via Veglia 18
St. Moritz
+41 81 836 80 00
kulm.com/en

The United Kingdom

The Connaught Bar
The Connaught Hotel
Carlos Place, Mayfair
London
+44 20 7499 7070
the-connaught.co.uk

Dukes Bar
35 St. James's Place
London
+44 20 7491 4840
dukeshotel.com/dukes-bar

St. John Bread and Wine
94-96 Commercial Street
Spitalfields
London
+44 20 7251 0848
stjohnrestaurant.com/pages/
bread-and-wine

The United States

Bar Pisellino
52 Grove Street
New York City
barpisellino.com

Café Altro Paradiso
234 Spring Street
New York City
646-952-0828
altroparadiso.com

Cafe Stella
3932 Sunset Boulevard
Los Angeles
323-666-0265
cafestella.com

Carbon Beach Club
Restaurant
Malibu Beach Inn
22878 Pacific Coast Highway
Malibu
310-460-7509
malibubeachinn.com

Dante
79-81 MacDougal Street
New York City
212-982-5275
dante-nyc.com

Eight Row Flint
1039 Yale Street
Houston
832-767-4002
agricolehospitality.com/
eight-row-flint

Franks Wine Bar
465 Court Street
Brooklyn, New York
718-254-0327
frankswinebar.com

Grand Army
336 State Street
Brooklyn, New York
718-643-1503
grandarmybar.com

Il Buco Alimentari & Vineria
53 Great Jones Street
New York City
212-837-2622
ilbuco.com/pages/alimentari

I Sodi
105 Christopher Street
New York City
212-414-5774
isodinyc.com

Jeffrey's Grocery
172 Waverly Place
New York City
646-398-7630
jeffreysgrocery.com

The Polo Bar
1 East 55th Street
New York City
212-207-8562
ralphlauren.com/
global-polo-bar

Quince
470 Pacific Avenue
San Francisco
415-775-8500
quincerestaurant.com

The Tower Bar
Sunset Tower Hotel
8358 Sunset Boulevard
West Hollywood
323-848-6677
sunsettowerhotel.com
/restaurants-and-bar/
tower-bar

The Duomo di Milano

FIAT
3388 FO

AFTERWORD

The best part about creating this book has been the extensive "research" involved. I've been very lucky to drink Negronis as I travel around the globe. I mostly stick to the classic, but I have been served a few variations that changed the way I feel about that now. Nevertheless, I have probably missed dozens of variations of the drink, in great places, created by talented barkeepers. Don't dismay, however; the research and development will continue.

The author at the end of a 2,000-mile road trip in his 1982 Fiat Panda

ACKNOWLEDGMENTS

I would like to thank my wife, Yolanda Edwards, who has supported me through every drink; my daughter, Clara, who tolerates my obsession; Linden Pride, Philip Williams, Matthew Karl-Gale, Damon Boelte, Frank Castronovo and Frank Falcinelli, Maurizio Stocchetto, Federico Morosi, Gerardo Cavaliere, Alessandro Palazzi, Alfio Liotta, Morgan Weber, Franck Audoux, Gabriel Stulman, and Tommy Martini, for our shared love of this drink; Ellen Morrissey, who helped so much shaping the content of this book; and my Artisan team: publisher Lia Ronnen, editor Shoshana Gutmajer, Elise Ramsbottom, Suet Chong, Nina Simoneaux, Sibylle Kazeroid, Barbara Peragine, Nancy Murray, Allison McGeehon, and Theresa Collier.

PANO
BRINDISI STORICO CON PUNT E MES
CARPANO
VERMUTH RE DAL 1786

CAMPARI
Bitter
G. Campari
... a base di
erbe
aromatiche
sceltissime
PIATTI

INDEX

Note: Page numbers in *italics* refer to illustrations.